WHO'S NEW?

by Anne O'Brien
illustrated by Theresa Burns

Harcourt

Orlando Boston Dallas Chicago San Diego

Visit *The Learning Site!*

www.harcourtschool.com

My name is Marcos. I have a new home in a new town in a new country. Everything is so different here. Will I like living in the United States?

Today is my first day in my new school. I feel nervous. Am I the only new student in my class? Who else is new?

My teacher introduces me to some students in my class. Ahmed and Isabel moved to this country last month. Jin Soo and Anya moved to this country last year.

They are all new, too! I'm so happy to meet them.

"Everything is so different here," I said. "Is this town like your old home?"

"This town is so small," Jin Soo said. "My old home was in an enormous city. Millions of people lived there."

"Oh, no," said Anya. "This town is so big. My old home was in a tiny village. I knew the names of everyone who lived there."

"This town is so wet," said Ahmed. "My old home was in the desert. It almost never rained there."

"Oh, no," said Isabel. "This town is so dry. My old home was in the rain forest. It rained almost every day there. The trees were always green."

"This town is so hot," said Anya. "My old home was in the north. We had cold, cold winters there. There was snow on the ground for most of the year."

"Oh, no," said Ahmed. "This town is so cold. My old home was in the south. It was very, very hot there."

"This town is so noisy," said Isabel. "My old home was in the country. All you heard was birds singing and tiny frogs peeping there."

"Oh, no," said Jin Soo. " This town is so quiet. My old home was next to a busy highway. You heard traffic all night long there. The sound helped me fall asleep."

"Wait!" I said, putting up my hands. "I think I understand now. My new home is small and big. It is very dry and very wet."

"My new home is hot and cold. It is also noisy and quiet. So my new home is everything all at once!" Everyone started laughing.

I think I am starting to like my new school in my new town in my new country. Can you guess what I like the most? I like the new friends I just met!